W9-CPF-698

ULTIMATE SCIENCE

PHYSICAL SCIENCE

Solids

Charlotte Deschermeier

PowerKiDS
press.

New York

Published in 2014 by The Rosen Publishing Group, Inc.
29 East 21st Street, New York, NY 10010

Library of Congress Cataloging-in-Publication Data

Deschermeier, Charlotte, author.
 Solids / by Charlotte Deschermeier.
    pages cm. – (Ultimate science. Physical science)
 Includes index.
 ISBN 978-1-4777-6003-1 (library) – ISBN 978-1-4777-6004-8 (pbk.) –
 ISBN 978-1-4777-6006-2 (6-pack)
 1. Solids–Juvenile literature. 2. Solid state physics–Juvenile literature. 3. Matter–Properties–
Juvenile literature. I. Title.
 QC176.3.D47 2014
 530.4'1–dc23
                          2013024010

Manufactured in the United States of America

CPSIA Compliance Information: Batch #W14PK4: For Further Information contact Rosen Publishing, New York, New York at 1-800-237-9932

Contents

Solids and Atoms

If you looked around, you would see that everything that surrounds you is made of matter. There are three basic states of matter. They are liquid, solid, and gas. Some solids are small, like a grain of sand. Other solids can be large, like a mountain. On Earth there are more solids than there are liquids or gases.

All matter is made of tiny particles, or parts, called atoms. Atoms join with other atoms to form **molecules**. The space between their molecules allows liquids and gas molecules to move freely.

Some solids are hard, like these stones. Others, like cotton balls, are softer.

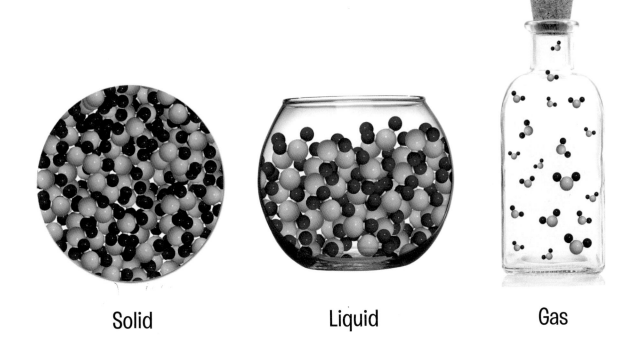

Solid   Liquid   Gas

However, in a solid, the molecules are tightly locked together. This **bond** prevents them from moving far, but they do **vibrate** in place. The forces of **attraction** between molecules are called intermolecular forces. Intermolecular forces hold the molecules together. The intermolecular forces, or bonds, are strongest in solids when compared to the other states of matter.

This picture shows the intermolecular forces in solids, liquids, and gases. Notice how much closer together the solid's molecules are than those in the liquid or gas.

olids Have No Flow

ot only are solid molecules tightly locked to each other, but they are also
ked close together. There is little space between them. The molecules in
olid have a greater attraction to each other than do those in a liquid or a
. If you spill a glass of liquid, such as water, it will spread across the table.
ou place a solid, such as a pebble, on the table, it will stay in one place.
will not drip off the table or become softer.

A mineral is a naturally occurring solid.
Quartz is one of the most common
minerals on Earth. Quartz is used to
make many man-made solids, such as
glass and special tools.

Unlike liquids, solids do not flow. The strong bonds, or intermolecular forces, in a solid hold it together and keep it from spreading. A solid keeps its shape. It does not have to be kept in a **container** like a liquid. Can you imagine what would happen if your chair was made of liquid?

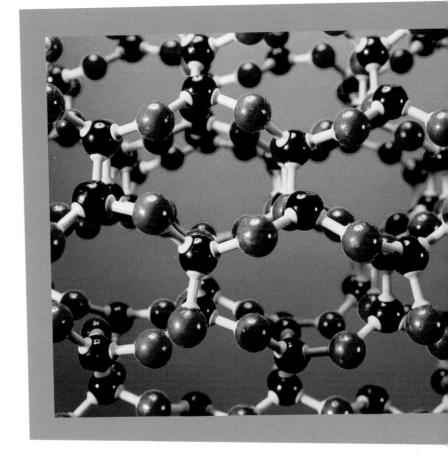

This is a model of a quartz molecule. The red balls are oxygen atoms, and the black balls are silicon atoms. The sticks joining these atoms stand for the bonds between them. Three silicon atoms and six oxygen atoms create a basic molecule of quartz.

Physical Properties of Solids

Physical **properties** are present in all matter. Size, shape, hardness, **texture**, and color are all examples of physical properties. We can use them to describe solids. Every pure solid also has a certain boiling point, melting point, and density. These are all physical properties, too. The physical properties of many solids are easy to see and describe.

Texture is one kind of physical property. Solids have different textures. Some solids, such as the metal bars on your bike, have a smooth texture. Other solids, such as your bike tire, feel bumpy.

Solids can be identified with the help of these physical properties. For example, physical properties can help a scientist tell the difference between two metals that look alike, like silver and nickel. By testing the hardness, density, and melting points, a scientist can easily tell which metal is nickel and which is silver. Solids have strong bonds. Liquids and gases have weaker ones. The strength of the intermolecular forces is another example of a physical property. The difference between different states of matter can be told with the help of physical properties.

Mineral	Hardness
Talc	1
Gypsum	2
Calcite	3
Fluorite	4
Apatite	5
Orthoclase	6
Quartz	7
Topaz	8
Corundum	9
Diamond	10

Hardness is a physical property that helps identify solids. Mohs' scale of hardness is a tool scientists use to test the hardness of different rocks and minerals. The softest rock is talc and the hardest is a diamond.

Solids and Shape

A solid can be of any size and shape. The shape of most solids cannot be changed. Both the strong intermolecular forces and the fixed pattern of molecules make it hard for solid molecules to rearrange themselves. Only fire or force will change a solid's shape.

Some solids are called crystals. A solid shaped like a crystal has its atoms or molecules arranged in a certain **geometric** pattern. The salt on your french fries and the sugar you put in cookies are two examples of solid crystals. Another crystal is diamond.

Table salt, which is magnified to 30 times its actual size here, has a crystal structure.

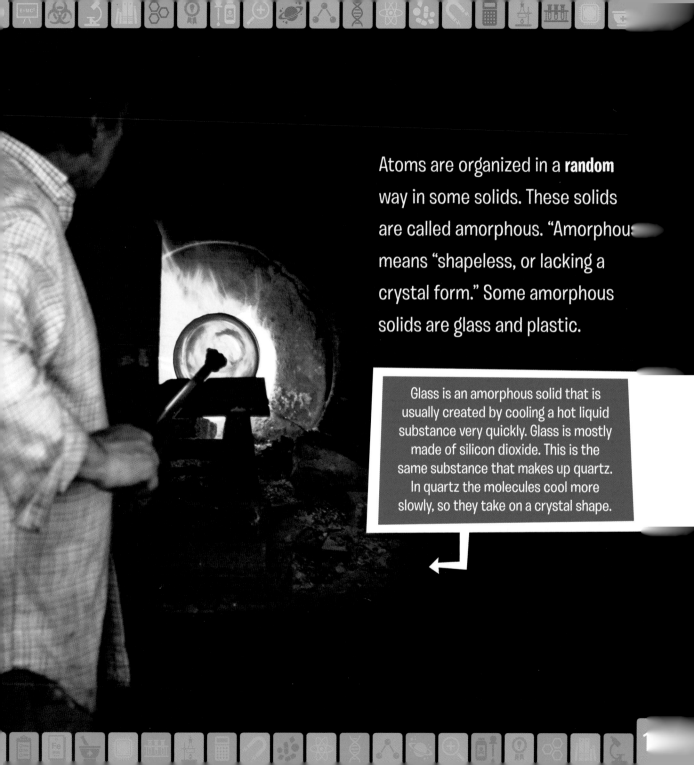

Atoms are organized in a **random** way in some solids. These solids are called amorphous. "Amorphous" means "shapeless, or lacking a crystal form." Some amorphous solids are glass and plastic.

Glass is an amorphous solid that is usually created by cooling a hot liquid substance very quickly. Glass is mostly made of silicon dioxide. This is the same substance that makes up quartz. In quartz the molecules cool more slowly, so they take on a crystal shape.

Solids and Volume

The amount of space that a **substance** takes up is its volume. Under ordinary conditions most solids keep their shape and take up a set amount of space. Liquids have volume, too, but they have no shape of their own. Gases have no fixed volume and no shape. They can be pressed into a very small space and will spread out as far as they can.

If you removed all the fish, plants, and rocks from this aquarium, the water level would go down. This is because these things all have volume and take up space in the aquarium.

Observing how much water is displaced, or moved, when the solid is placed in a large glass tube is one way of measuring a solid's volume. The change in the water level tells us the object's volume. Think about the amount of space a whale takes up. Now picture a scuba diver who takes up much less space than the whale. Do you think the scuba diver or the whale will displace more water? Based on this, what observation can you make about each one's volume?

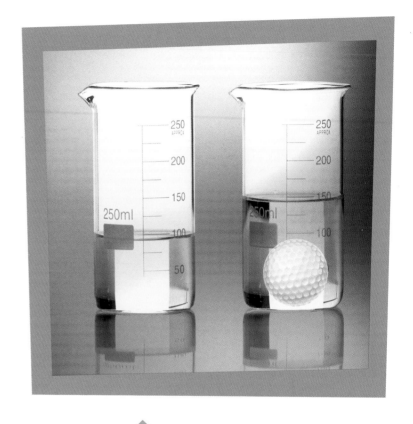

Here, two glasses hold the same amount of water. A golf ball has been dropped into the glass on the right. By measuring the difference in the water level, we can find the volume of the golf ball.

Solids and Density

Density is present in all solids. It tells you how tightly packed the molecules are in a solid. The closer the molecules are to each other, the denser a substance is. If two solids of the same volume have different densities, the one that is denser will feel heavier. Of the three most common states of matter on Earth, solids are usually the densest.

Metals are usually dense solids, with a lot of weight at small volumes. If an anchor were made out of wood or some less dense substance, it would not be able to hold a boat firmly in place.

Did you know that the ability of a solid to sink or float depends on its density? For example, cork is less dense than water. Cork will float to the water's surface. An anchor, which is often made of a metal such as steel, is denser than water. Therefore, the anchor will sink to the bottom of the water.

A crew at sea will tie a heavy anchor to their ship and then drop the anchor into the water. The ship is kept from drifting by the anchor.

Cork is made from the bark of a cork tree. Cork has many air pockets. These air pockets make cork less dense than water.

Freezing and Melting Solids

Matter changes its state sometimes. For example, a liquid can turn into a solid if it becomes cold enough. This is called freezing. The **temperature** at which a substance becomes a solid is called its freezing point. Different liquids become solid at different freezing points. Liquid water becomes solid ice at 32°F (0°C). When water freezes it takes up more space. Have you ever made your own popsicles with juice? Most of juice is water.

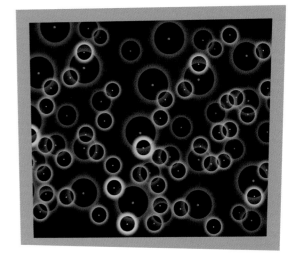

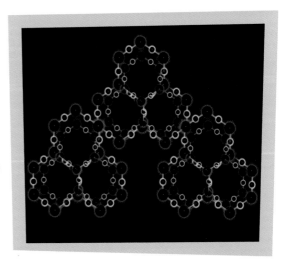

On the top is a picture of water molecules in liquid form. On the bottom is water as ice. The molecules in the liquid have no special arrangement. The ones in the ice have an orderly, crystal structure.

The juice will spill out if you fill a popsicle tray to the top. This is because the water in the juice takes up more space when it freezes.

A solid will change into a liquid if it is heated to a high enough temperature. Changing from a solid to a liquid is called melting. The temperature at which this occurs is a solid's melting point. When a solid reaches its melting point, its molecules unlock and begin to move freely. It then becomes a liquid.

Chocolate has a relatively low melting point. It is around 97°F (36°C). At this temperature, chocolate becomes a liquid.

Changing from a Solid to a Gas

Usually, before turning into a gas, a solid turns into a liquid. However, some solids change directly into gases. This process is called sublimation. A solid called dry ice can change into a gas. Dry ice is frozen carbon dioxide. Dry ice does not melt. Instead it sublimes into carbon dioxide gas. Have you watched a play that had fog or mist on the stage? The spooky scene may have been created by using dry ice.

During sublimation a solid turns directly into a gas. Molecules of the solid break free from the solid's surface, as shown in this picture.

ome molecules escape the strong intermolecular forces and enter he air as gas molecules when a solid sublimates. At the same time, other gas molecules floating above the solid **collide** with the solid's surface and return to the solid state. This is called **deposition**.

Unlike ice made from water, ice from carbon dioxide does not go through a liquid stage under normal conditions. This is why it is called dry ice.

Solids and Mixtures

Elements are substances that are made from only one kind of atom. Most matter, including most solids, is a combination of two or more elements. This is called a mixture. In a mixture each substance keeps its original physical properties. This means that mixtures can be separated back into the solids, liquids, or gases that created them. For example, if you mixed pretzels and peanuts as a snack, you could separate each kind of food again.

Sand

Clay

Silt

A mixture can be made from two solids. Soil, a mixture of rocks and minerals, is a solid-solid mixture. Here, three different kinds of soil are shown. **Top:** Sand has larger pieces than silt does. **Left:** Clay often has water mixed in with the pieces of rock. **Right:** Silt is a fine mixture of tiny pieces of rock and sediment.

When a solid **dissolves** in a liquid, the kind of mixture created is called a solution. For example, when you dissolve sugar and cocoa in hot milk you make a solution of hot chocolate. The substances that dissolve in the liquid are called solutes. The solutes in hot chocolate are sugar and cocoa. The liquid in which the solute is dissolved is called the solvent. Milk is the solvent in a hot chocolate solution. Some solids will not dissolve in liquids. Such solids are known as insoluble.

Some solutions can be made from a liquid and a solid. Pour a spoonful of sugar into a cup of tea, and you've made a solid-liquid solution.

Solids Really Matter

The book you are reading, the chair you are sitting on, and even some of the food you ate at your last meal are all solids. There's no doubt about it, solids play an important part in our lives.

Solids will last for a long time and will not change much over time. Solids in the form of million-year-old **fossils** have been found by scientists in many places throughout the world. The fossils allow scientists to see what life was like long ago.

It's hard to imagine a world without solids. Without them there would be no trees or flowers, no houses, no schools, and no hospitals. Without solids there would be no life. So we can see that solids really matter!

Glossary

attraction (uh-TRAK-shun) Pulling something together or toward something else.

bond (BOND) What holds two things together.

collide (kuh-LYD) Crash together.

container (kun-TAY-ner) Something that holds things.

deposition (deh-puh-ZIH-shun) The way in which molecules in a gaseous state become a solid.

dissolves (dih-ZOLVZ) Breaks down.

elements (EH-luh-ments) The basic matter of which all things are made.

fossils (FAH-sulz) The hardened remains of a dead animal or plant.

geometric (jee-uh-MEH-trik) Having to do with straight lines, circles, and other simple shapes.

molecules (MAH-lih-kyoolz) Two or more atoms joined together.

physical properties (FIH-zih-kul PRAH-per-teez) The features or characteristics of a certain substance.

random (RAN-dum) Having no set pattern or order.

substance (SUB-stans) Any matter that takes up space.

temperature (TEM-pur-cher) How hot or cold something is.

texture (TEKS-chur) How something feels when you touch it.

vibrate (VY-brayt) To move back and forth quickly.

Index

Websites

Due to the changing nature of Internet links, PowerKids Press has developed an online list of websites related to the subject of this book. This site is updated regularly. Please use this link to access the list:

www.powerkidslinks.com/usps/solids/